147 Practical Tips
for Using Icebreakers
with College Students

By
Robert Magnan

Atwood Publishing
Madison, WI

147 Practical Tips for Using Icebreakers with College Students
By Robert Magnan

© 2005, Atwood Publishing, Madison, WI
www. atwoodpublishing.com

Cover design by Tamara Dever, TLC Graphics
www.tlcgraphics.com

Library of Congress Cataloging-in-Publication Data

Magnan, Robert.
  147 practical tips for using icebreakers with college students / by Robert
Magnan.
     p. cm.
  ISBN 1-891859-57-9 (pbk.)
  1. College teaching—United States. 2. Classroom environment—United
States. 3. College students—United States—Psychology. 4. Learning,
Psychology of. I. Title: One hundred forty-seven practical tips for using
icebreakers with college students. II. Title.

  LB2331.M346 2005
  378.1'2—dc22
                              2005002121

Acknowledgments

I would like to thank Linda Babler of Atwood Publishing for persuading me to write this book — 15 years after I wrote *147 Practical Tips for Teaching Professors*. It didn't take much persuasion, actually, and I truly enjoyed the experience. Thanks too to Kristin Wieben, her assistant.

I would also like to thank Katy J. Vopal, with whom this manuscript traveled across three states as she read it with interest and provided valuable insights and suggestions for improving it —as well as lots of encouragement and a few reality checks. She even thanked me for sharing it with her! You and I owe Katy J. a debt of gratitude. As I read her comments, I felt like she and I were talking over coffee between classes, enthusiastic about the possibilities. I have only one regret about involving her in this project — that I didn't do it earlier.

In addition, I would like to thank my cousin, Laura Nicole Magnan, for being inspirational, and her mother, Mandy Hauschild Magnan, for reviewing the manuscript.

And last here but first of all in my life, I thank my earliest teacher — Barbara Knowlton Magnan, my mother.

Table of Contents

Introduction

What is an icebreaker? This term is a label for various activities used by instructors, trainers, and facilitators to help the members of a group feel comfortable, to promote interaction, to help them form bonds and work together, to stimulate creative thinking, and to energize them.

The term "icebreaker" may make us think of those boats that keep shipping lanes open in cold weather. However, the origin of the term seems to be much older.

Since the beginnings of the human race, people who lived in colder climates had to break through the ice of rivers, ponds, or wells in order to draw water. Also, people who relied on boats for transportation would find it necessary to use axes and other tools to break ice in front of their boats in order to row, pole, or sail their crafts. So, breaking the ice, from the beginning, meant removing an obstacle that would prevent drawing something vital to life or making necessary progress toward a destination.

From those origins, the term "icebreaker" has evolved to include any techniques that help remove obstacles to communicating and connecting in social situations. Icebreakers help people meet at parties or in bars. Icebreakers help trainers and facilitators connect with participants in training sessions, workshops, seminars, and conferences. Because icebreakers help to bring people together, to create bonds and a sense of community, it's an appropriate term for "welcome and warm-up exercises" that we can use with our students at the start of a course.

When I was writing this book, I asked my cousin Laura Nicole about ways to welcome students into a course. She suggested passing out cookies, having a class picnic, and going outside to stretch and do jumping jacks in the fresh air. Good ideas! However, in this book, icebreakers are limited to activities that can be done within the learning environment, whether in a room or online.

I should also mention a few things about the terms used in this book. By "board" I mean generally a blackboard, an overhead transparency, an electronic whiteboard, or any other display that the students can view in class. By "classroom" I mean generally the area in which you and your students meet for the course, whether a conventional classroom, a laboratory, an auditorium, a field site, or a virtual setting.

Why Icebreakers?

The primary goal for an icebreaker is to begin developing an environment that is comfortable and conducive to learning, especially through interactions among students. Angela Provitera McGlynn puts it well in her book, *Successful Beginnings for College Teaching* (pp. 35, 52):

> The first class meeting of the semester is the most important one of the term! It sets the tone for the entire course — for better or worse. ...

> Staring the semester with *icebreakers* and other activities to get students comfortable in the classroom is becoming more widely accepted, as the research piles up showing the importance of helping students bond with their classmates so that they stay in school and graduate. ...

> The goal is to start the semester by developing a relaxed learning atmosphere. Students want the classroom to be safe and friendly.

An icebreaker can be vital to feeling a sense of community and collaboration in a class. This is especially important in larger classes. Many icebreakers are more appropriate for smaller classes, but some are included here for larger classes and there are some tips for adapting other icebreakers to make them work for larger classes.

Icebreakers can be even more important in online courses, where a sense of community is generally more difficult to form — and even more vital for some students because of their social needs. Most icebreakers are designed for face-to-face environments. But generally, any icebreaker that can be modified to work mainly with text-based dialogue can succeed in an online course.

Most of the icebreakers to be found in books, in articles, and on Web pages are intended for elementary and secondary teachers and for trainers and facilitators. Relatively few college and university instructors use icebreakers, and they're used more often by instructors in community colleges than by instructors in four-year schools.

So, why are icebreakers less common in postsecondary education?

It seems to be a logical corollary of the traditional continuum of education from student-centered to subject-centered. At the lowest level of education, the teacher focuses mostly on the students; then, the higher the level, the more the focus shifts from students to subject. Consequently, to put it simplistically, in early elementary the teachers work hardest at reaching the students and helping them understand the subject matter, but by college the instructors expect the students to assume much more responsibility for learning.

Consequently, in college, instructors and/or students generally consider icebreakers unnecessary—or at least feel like that's the natural and normal expectation. After all, the students are adults: they should assume the responsibility of getting to know each other and of being prepared to start the course. Helping them do so is not a significant part of teaching, which is focused on the subject matter and not on the students.

So, at that level, instructors and students may consider icebreakers a little beneath their dignity. Of course, both the instructors and the students should be serious about their courses. However, it could be argued that people tend to learn better and more easily if they feel at ease — not stressed ... and certainly not bored.

Furthermore, from this conventional perspective of focusing on the subject and not the students, instructors and students may feel that icebreakers take too much time, in terms of return on investment. Even a short activity, perhaps five minutes, means that five minutes of class time is not being devoted to the course material. (However, it could be argued that spending a little time to help students feel comfortable would be a wise investment in the course.)

But the perspective of the traditional continuum clashes with reality. As Joseph Lowman observes in *Mastering the Techniques of Teaching* (2nd edition) (San Francisco: Jossey-Bass, 2000):

> In theory, the college classroom is strictly an intellectual and rational setting. In reality, a classroom is an emotionally charged interpersonal arena in which a wide range of psychological phenomena occur... College classrooms ... are complex interpersonal arenas in which a variety of emotional reactions

can influence how much is learned and how the participants feel about it. (pp. 26, 27)

Lowman emphasizes the importance of developing rapport with the students. He concludes, "Anything you can do to show interest in students as individuals will help to promote rapport" (p. 72)

This is not primarily a collection of icebreakers. The purpose of this book is to help college and university instructors use icebreakers in their teaching. It offers suggestions for choosing icebreakers and getting the greatest benefits from using them.

This book describes more than 60 icebreakers and offers 147 tips for choosing and using them. Think of them as a selection of basic, all-occasion recipes with serving suggestions and alternative possibilities. These icebreakers are appropriate for one or more of the purposes outlined above and for courses in various subject areas. The examples were selected because they are simple and appropriate for adults and because they represent a wide range of possibilities. The focus of an icebreaker at the college and university level should be on the students and the instructor, not the activity itself. Therefore, although most of the tips relate to specific icebreakers, many apply in general to choosing and using icebreakers.

This book will not try to convince you to try icebreakers with your students. The primary objective of this book is to show how icebreakers can work and the purposes for choosing and using them. The icebreakers presented here and the tips for adapting them to different situations and purposes are intended to help instructors who have good intentions and want to try icebreakers.

Now, you may be thinking, "I'd like to try using an icebreaker, but ...." OK, so why are you hesitant?

Some instructors may feel that icebreakers might not work in their courses. If you feel that way, we hope that this book will change your mind.

Some instructors tend to be introverted and would feel less comfortable with using icebreakers than their more extroverted colleagues. If you feel that way, here's the first tip — a bonus in addition to the 147 promised in the title ....

TIP: Expand your comfort zone.

Try using icebreakers! If you expect your students to work beyond their areas of comfort, you can serve as an example.

Some instructors want to use icebreakers, but don't know where to begin. So, we have the next bonus tip ...

TIP: Know what you want the icebreaker to do.

What is the purpose for the icebreaker? Why are you using an icebreaker? What changes do you want? How do you want your students to feel and act as a result? Don't use them just to soften the start of classes.

That's the first step in choosing an icebreaker. That's why the icebreakers and the tips in this book are divided into sections, according to the following basic purposes for icebreakers:

- to help your students feel comfortable
- to introduce yourself to your students
- to get a sense of your students in general
- to make it easier for your students to get to know each other
- to encourage your students to share and explore their differences
- to establish an active, participatory environment by getting the students working together, in pairs or small groups
- to bring out feelings about the subject and the course, to lead students into the course, and to generate interest
- to encourage students to be interested in each other, to share information and resources, and to identify their individual needs and goals
- to foster comfort and confidence in a virtual community

This organization by purposes is intended to make it easier for you to choose an icebreaker appropriate to your purpose. You could also select two or more icebreakers, for a series of purposes.

Also, although the icebreakers in this book are organized into categories according to purposes, some of them could easily be used for other purposes than the one for which they're designated here. As with any other teaching technique, it's not just about purpose. You should also consider other factors, including these:

- subject of your course

- level of your course
- setting and/or format of your course
- ages of your students
- experiences and backgrounds of your students
- attitudes of your students
- you — how you think and feel as an instructor an a person

The *subject* of your course is a crucial consideration. Many subjects offer good possibilities for icebreakers. However, choosing an icebreaker can be more problematic when the students are not comfortable in the language. This is the case in beginning foreign language courses taught in the target language or courses in English as a second language (ESL, a.k.a. English for speakers of other languages, English as a foreign language, and English for academic purposes). In these situations, many students might feel uncomfortable starting in situations that require them to use the language they're learning. For such situations, there are activities that are easy to explain and in which the students communicate more nonverbally and speak less.

The *level* of your course could make a difference in how you choose and use icebreakers. It could be difficult with students who are older, at least several years out of high school — situations in which students may react to icebreakers in terms of their experiences in middle or junior high and high school, years past. For such situations, there are activities that engage the students more intellectually, perhaps involving use of the subject matter, perhaps encouraging them to share more of their academic, career, or life experiences.

The *setting and/or format* of your course may make some icebreakers more effective — or make some very difficult or even impossible. You may not be teaching in a conventional classroom; you may have to adapt an icebreaker to an auditorium or a laboratory. There are activities that work well with larger classes and activities that don't require the students to move around. It would also be very difficult in courses taught through cable or closed-circuit TV — situations in which communication is not two-way. For such situations, there are activities that focus on interaction among the students and do not involve the instructor.

The *ages* of your students may also be important. A mix of students straight out of high school and students who are five, 10, 20, or more years older can make it more difficult to use some icebreakers. This is also true when the *experiences and backgrounds* of your students vary greatly. An extreme case might be courses in English as a second language, in which cultural diversity might inhibit interaction, especially for students from cultures where students are expected to learn passively, without participating actively. For such situations, there are activities that encourage students to share information about themselves, to bring out differences from the start, openly.

The most important factor is likely to be the attitudes of your students, which may include any of the following possibilities:

- interest
- enthusiasm
- anxiety
- fear
- apathy
- resistance
- boredom
- timidity
- annoyance

We all appreciate the first two attitudes — interest and enthusiasm — in our students. But the other attitudes might make us hesitate to try something different in the classroom, such as icebreakers. It's naturally difficult to take chances when you anticipate that your students may react to an icebreaker with the following thoughts:

- "Huh? I don't get it!" (Some students may miss the point of the icebreaker, not understand the purpose.)
- "Uh ... um ...." (Students may be turned off, annoyed, made uncomfortable by the exercise. In other words, the icebreaker chills the environment and thickens the ice.)
- "What a waste!" (Students may feel that the benefits of the icebreaker, whatever they may be, are not worth the time and/or effort.)
- "Time for teacher to show off!" (Some students may feel that an icebreaker seems to be more about the instructor than about the students.)
- "Why should I care about the other students? I'm here to learn from somebody who knows something — or at least to get a grade. So the only person who matters is the instructor!"

(Many students show little interest when their classmates ask a question or contribute to a discussion.)

- "Ho-hum." (Some students may not show any interest in anything — especially if the course is required.)
- "Eeeewwww. Uh, I don't think so." (Some students may express an extreme, apprehensive or scornful reaction to something that seems too "touchy-feely" or "warm and fuzzy.")
- "Whatever." (The all-purpose, one-size-fits-all reaction that expresses nothing specifically.)

So why should the introduction to a book on choosing and using icebreakers, a book that promotes the benefits of icebreakers, describe a range of possible negative reactions? Because many instructors fail to try icebreakers because they feel anxious about these possibilities.

TIP: Don't expect negative reactions, but anticipate the possibilities.

Be attentive to any signs — but not pessimistically or with a sense of dread. Expecting negative reactions can cause instructors to be nervous and/or to not commit emotionally to making an icebreaker work. As with any teaching technique or exercise, plan for it to work — and be ready to handle any difficulties.

Keep in mind the advice of Katy J. Vopal, who teaches writing, literature, and public speaking at Lakeland College: "The instructor should gauge the majority of the students. Don't decide not to do an icebreaker because you have one or two 'eye rollers.' There are always a couple of students who don't like anything. I find that, while the group may be resistant to an icebreaker at first, afterwards they see the value and importance of the exercise."

Two Big Questions and a Tough Decision

By this point, you may be wondering, "I'm worried about taking risks with icebreakers with my students. Is it worth it? If so, what can I do to reduce the risks and maximize the benefits?"

Two good questions. The first — Is it worth it? — only you can answer — and only after you use icebreakers with your students. The second — What can I do? — we hope to answer in this book.

But here's the short answer. You make tough decisions about your students when you plan your course and when you plan each class, when you select strategies and techniques for teaching, when you create tests and exams, and when you evaluate your students. So, think about your course and your students and your purposes for using an icebreaker. Then, try to remain flexible and open to whatever happens.

The icebreakers you choose and the ways you use them send messages to your students about you, how you understand them, how you approach teaching and learning, and how you feel about beginning the course. An icebreaker is a great opportunity to welcome your students into your course and warm them up to each other and to you.

It's very important, then, to choose and use icebreakers appropriately. Only you know your situation and your needs, so only you can make the best decision when choosing icebreakers. I hope that this book will help you.

Good luck!

Category: General Tips

PURPOSE: to help your students feel comfortable

Most people feel at least a little anxious about new situations. That's especially true for students, because with each course they're entering into a situation that will test — literally and figuratively — their intelligence, knowledge, and memory, an environment in which they will be judged and evaluated — not only by an instructor but also by their classmates. So, the icebreakers in this section will help lower your students' anxiety levels.

1. Understand the anxiety that some students feel.

Occasionally, it's even fear. Some instructors believe that the anxiety and the fear are of them, the instructors. That's not quite it — not completely. Students are also anxious and fearful of each other. Many don't want to stand out in the class — especially for saying things, giving answers, and asking questions that might cause others to consider them stupid or uncool. So, an icebreaker that you feel will be fun for all may not turn out that way for some students. Think back to when you were a student beginning a course. Or just think as far back as attending your first faculty meeting. Even though you probably knew at least some of your colleagues and knew that they had to treat you at least civilly in meetings, you may have been anxious about not looking like a fool. So, let any memories of anxiety and fear guide you in choosing and using icebreakers to ensure a comfortable environment for all of your students. If in doubt, pick an activity that's simple and avoids personal issues or physical activity.

2. Let them know your intentions.

With the exception of a few icebreakers that depend on an element of surprise, you should explain what you're doing before you start an activity, e.g., "I thought that it might help all of us feel more comfortable here if we started with a little activity that I hope will be fun" or "Since I don't know any of you and you don't know me, it might be good to begin the term with an introductory exercise."

3. Balance fun and function.

Depending on your students, the subject, and the level of anxiety you expect, the icebreakers that you use might be heavily functional or more on the fun side. Keep that balance in mind as you read this book.

4. Think about tone.

This icebreaker will probably be the first connection that you make with your students. A more serious icebreaker may send a message that your course may not be very enjoyable. On the other hand, a silly icebreaker may cause students to assume that they can take a casual attitude toward your course. It can be a tough call. How have students reacted to the course in the past, with you or with colleagues? If they seemed anxious or even afraid, then it may be better to err on the side of fun. If they seemed too relaxed — attendance problems, inadequate effort on assignments, insufficient preparation for quizzes and exams — then you could start out better with a more serious icebreaker, preferably focused on the course content.

5. Keep your icebreakers short.

Many students, especially nontraditional ones, are serious about being in college, especially if this is their first term. They may be anxious about spending any time on activities off the subject. Focus on helping your students feel comfortable. Don't get too ambitious: unless your class is small, the students won't all have a chance to meet each other. Just make a start and then let time do the rest. If you involve the students in your teaching methods, through discussions and group activities, they'll get to know each other naturally.

6. Keep your icebreakers simple and easy to understand.

Simpler is usually better, as long as the icebreaker is not so basic and common that it bores the students to tears. The more elaborate the activity, the more the fun-function balance may seem tipped. If you can't explain an activity in a few sentences, it may be too complicated for the benefits and it's likely to take more time than it's worth. Students usually don't want to risk appearing to be too stupid to understand how a game works.

7. Give directions, provide guidelines, and express your expectations — in advance.

Then, always ask your students what questions they have before they begin. Assume that there are questions; asking, "Do you have any questions?" tends to encourage most students to keep silent or maybe just shake their heads. If nobody asks any questions, ask one or two yourself, such as "So, when I say ..., what do you do?"

For example, if the activity involves having your students introduce themselves, one by one, if you don't let them know what you expect, it's likely that the first student will set a pattern that many of the others will follow. So, if the first student only gives his or her name, the rest of the introductions are likely to follow suit, which may not be what you wanted. If the first student stops short, gently prompt him or her to elaborate. Usually the students following will take the cue and not oblige you to prompt them for more.

8. Set a length.

Introductions can vary greatly in detail and, consequently, duration. If you don't tell the students what you expect, they're likely to play follow the leader. So, if the first student delivers a five-minute autobiography, some of the others may do the same ... and many may feel uncomfortable because they don't want to talk for that long. Plus, long introductions take a lot of time and may be tiring after a while. So, suggest a length in time ("Take a minute or two to tell us about yourself") or in words ("Tell us about yourself in 50 words, more or less"). Then provide an example, introducing yourself in a minute or two or in 50 words, more or less. Don't let any students go on and on and on. The others are likely to become restless and even resentful. Limit the loquacious, gently, just as you lead out the laconic. Some may feel embarrassed at first, but if you keep the activity going, the feelings won't last. Besides, at some point in the course you'll probably have to discourage some students from dominating discussion, so why not do it right ... from the start?

9. Don't gamble with games.

Most adults consider themselves too old and/or sophisticated to be playing games in a classroom. So, if you use a game as an icebreaker, you should consider either keeping it short or planning for a quick ending in case it isn't working very well. Give it a chance, of course, but don't push it.

10. Don't try too hard to be different.

Sometimes something different can be refreshing, even invigorating ... and sometimes it can be just different, even weird. Creativity counts ... but only if it makes an icebreaker more effective. Originality is of some value in using an icebreaker, but your purpose should be to make the students feel more comfortable — not to entertain them and certainly not to confuse or overwhelm or stress them. You want to help the students step out of their comfort zone — not to shrink those comfort zones.

11. Break some ice on your own.

If you've gotten into the habit of using the same icebreaker course after course, break through the ice of habit and try something different! If you're expecting your students to take risks from the start, you should be taking risks too.

12. Make it unique.

Whatever icebreaker you choose, it's possible, even probable, that some of the students will have been through it before. How do you avoid the feeling of "Been there, done that"?

13. Involve subject matter or skills relevant to the course — if appropriate.

If you don't know of any icebreakers designed for your subject area, modify generic icebreakers. There are tips on doing so throughout this book.

14. Showcase the "real-life" knowledge of your students.

Questions about the community or the campus are good, especially as they can help students begin trusting each other as valuable resources. Most students would be interested in good pizzerias, fun places to bike, inexpensive movies, and so forth. With nontraditional students, you might ask about careers, families, travel, and hobbies.

15. Allow an "out" if students feel uncomfortable.

Since one of the basic purposes of any icebreaker is to help the students feel comfortable with each other and with you, why undermine your efforts with questions or other activities that might make students feel less comfortable? It might be best to simply avoid some questions and activities, so students don't feel caught between the embarrassment of saying or doing something they don't want to and the embarrassment of opting out of a question or an activity.

16. Avoid getting too "up close and personal."

Even if you believe that all or most of the students will feel comfortable answering personal questions about themselves, think about how the they might feel hearing the answers about others. What happens if a student reveals more than others are able to accept comfortably?

17. Answer every question yourself — at least a dozen ways.

Some students might take the opportunity of icebreaker questions to show off or to shock. It's not common in postsecondary environments, but it happens. Questions such as "What activity did you enjoy most in high school?" or "What's your most important reason for choosing this school?" might lead the students to answer — seriously or jokingly — with comments that might offend others. If you consider the probable directions that answers might take, you can eliminate a lot of potential problems.

Katy J. Vopal once did an icebreaker in which she asked her students to list things they considered *exciting*. All of the students in that class were male — and the items they listed quickly focused on women, specifically on body parts. As she notes, "If you let unruly or inappropriate behavior go, especially during an icebreaker, it can set a bad tone or make students uncomfortable for a long time."

18. Be careful with creativity.

It's tempting to use icebreakers that require or encourage students to be creative. After all, when such activities work, they generate enthusiasm and increase interactivity. However, they also may create pressure on some students, by putting them on the spot in what feels like a "creativity competition." It's usually wiser to simply provide an opportunity for students to show their individuality; some will be more creative than others, but the others will likely feel less pressure.

19. Always be sensitive to your students.

Be aware of their different levels of comfort and stay within their comfort zones.

However, don't let any social, educational, cultural, or other differences within your class keep you from helping your students gain new insights. It's appropriate at times to encourage students to expand their comfort zones — but generally not during icebreakers. At the beginning of the course, for most students, the environment will not be conducive to taking chances.

20. Check this list before choosing an icebreaker.

- Could this activity embarrass any students?
- Does this activity require an environment of greater trust for all students to participate?
- Could any students fail at something that they're expected to do in the activity?
- Could this activity cause discomfort rather than increasing comfort?
- If the answer to any of these questions is "Yes," this icebreaker may not be appropriate for your students.

21. Be honest ... and be human.

Give the icebreaker time to work. However, if an icebreaker doesn't seem to be working, stop and open up with your students. "Well, this activity isn't going as well as I'd hoped? So, what am I doing wrong? What would work better to help all of you feel more comfortable here?" The students should appreciate that you can recognize and admit to problems and that you want to work with them to resolve problems. That's important for them to know. Sometimes good things come of failures. On the other hand, if your students aren't participating as you expected, it may be that they don't want to do anything, including answering questions about the activity. If that seems to be the case, you might try converting the icebreaker to a pen-and-paper exercise.

Category: Who Am I?

PURPOSE: to introduce yourself to your students

What's most on the minds of students as they start a course is the instructor. You're the boss, you're the judge, you're the guide. The students want to know about you, the great unknown variable in the educational equation. And they probably want to know more than your name, office number, office hours, and office phone number. The icebreakers here will help show that you're a person, not just an educational function.

MEET AND GREET

This simple icebreaker comes from Stephen Steele of Anne Arundel Community College (American Sociological Association, www.asanet.org/apap/classideas.html). It's his favorite:

Walk among the students and introduce yourself and shake hands. Ask their names "and greet them as personally as possible." Steele adds, "They might even feel like humans .... Most of the learners I've had in 31 years of teaching are absolutely shocked ... but pleased ... shocked because no one had ever done this."

22. Greet and meet at the door.

This icebreaker is great — but it might not work as well if you've got a larger class or the seating makes it more difficult to move around among the students. In that case, stand just outside or inside the door and welcome your students as they arrive. This can be difficult if they arrive in clusters, as is often the case close to class time. But if you block the entrance slightly, you can shape a cluster into a line and meet every student one on one.

JUST ONE OF THEM

Arrive 10 minutes early and sit among the students: be "just one of them." When the class is scheduled to begin, leave your seat and go to the front of the room. At the very least, this unorthodox beginning will generate reactions. You can probe those reactions and encourage discussion. Why do they feel the way they feel? You could mention that one theory about learning is that it results when the intellectual equilibrium is disturbed, creating cognitive dissonance. So how was their equilibrium disturbed? What did they learn? How are things different now? What expectations do students have of their instructors and their courses? It's OK if the students don't have any answers or if they don't seem interested in discussing the questions. Some questions are more effective than answers.

23. Foil their expectations only to create a teachable moment.

Don't use this icebreaker only for shock value. I know someone who tried this strategy, "going undercover" as a way to reduce or remove the usual barrier between student and instructors — and some students were very bothered by what they considered a trick or a deception, as if the instructor had gone undercover to spy on them. This tactic might work best in psychology or sociology, but unless a discussion of the "covert presence" and their reactions would be relevant to the course, this tactic might be inappropriate as an icebreaker and even compromise the environment.

WHAT I WANT TO KNOW

Invite the students to write down on a slip of paper one thing that they would like to know about the course, about you, about the subject matter in general, about careers in the field, and so forth. Collect those slips. Then, read each question and try to answer it.

24. Keep the Q&A light and bright.

This activity not only encourages the students to ask questions in your course and provides them with answers, but also shows how you will deal with questions. So, take the serious questions seriously, but keep it casual and comfortable. You don't need to be Jay Leno or David

Letterman answering questions from the studio audience, but it should move easily and quickly.

Katy J. Vopal suggests having the students sign their question slips, because "an opportunity to ask questions anonymously could lead to humiliating questions." Of course, you could also just skip questions that you consider inappropriate; just comment, "That's a little personal at this point" and pass to the next question.

25. Be honest.

Don't hesitate to admit that you don't have an answer. Promise to get back to the class with the answer — and then do it, as soon as possible. In some ways, you can impress your students more by admitting to not knowing and then finding out than if you knew all the answers — and far more than if you tried to talk around the issue.

26. Have the students stand and deliver.

Each student reads his or her questions. This gets them speaking out from the very start, but that means that some may not dare ask all the questions they have — and maybe the most important.

27. Pass into anonymity.

Have the students pass their slips of paper from one to another, several times, until nobody knows whose questions are in whose hand. Then have the students ask the questions they're holding. Some may still hesitate to speak out, but they will be more likely to ask all of the questions, because they come from other students.

No Jeopardy

Prepare a list of things that have some significance to you — colors, names, places, dates, etc. Write one of these items on the board. For example, "orange." Then, invite the students to guess at the significance by asking questions that could be answered by the item. For example: What's your favorite fruit? What color is your car? What's your favorite color? What color do you never wear? What county did you visit on your last vacation?

28. Turn the activity over to the students.

Have each student, one by one, come to the board and write an item that has some significance for him or her. The other students guess, again in the form of questions. Students who spend some time up in front during the first class are less likely to try to avoid participating in activities. Start with volunteers, so those who are shy can prepare for the experience.

Category: Who Are You?

PURPOSE: to get a sense of your students in general

You may be merely curious about your students — or you may be wondering about how you can most effectively help them learn. There are fewer and fewer classes in which all of the students are of traditional age with conventional experiences. Also, if the course is relatively new or you're relatively new to teaching the course, you may be wondering whether you've prepared appropriately and whether your plans and approaches and techniques will be suitable. So, for many reasons, you may want to get a general sense of your students. That's the primary purpose of the icebreakers in this section.

SURVEY

Survey the class with some questions about their backgrounds and academic situations. Ask them to raise a hand to any question that applies to them. For example:

- How many of you were born in this city or the surrounding area?
- How many of you come from outside this state?
- How many of you were born outside the United States?
- How many of you are first-year students? Sophomores? Juniors? Seniors?
- How many of you are majoring in ...? (Name areas related to the course subject.)
- How many of you have taken ...? (Name courses related to your course.)

This activity gives the students a general overview of the other students in the class and it allows you to get a better sense of the needs and interests of your students.

29. Get relevant with caution.

Questions about knowledge of the subject matter and experience in the area can be risky. Make them interesting, but keep them from encouraging competition. The benefit of this activity for the students is that they will feel a sense of community. However, if the survey touches on individual academic achievements that could make the environment more competitive than cooperative and collaborative, the benefit becomes a disadvantage for at least some of the students. For example, the question "Who has a GPA of 3.9 or higher?" would not help any students know each other better; it would only cause feelings of superiority in some and insecurity in others.

SURVEY BY SUGGESTIONS

Ask your students what they want to know about each other. Pass out index cards and ask the students to write down a yes-or-no question for you to ask. You can request that they limit their questions to academic matters — this course, their expectations, their related interests, and so forth, such as "Are you majoring in physics?" or "Are you taking this course only because it's required?" — or you can allow them total freedom. Collect their questions and then read them one by one, asking the students to raise a hand to any question to which they would answer yes.

30. Keep track of the results.

Ask a student to write on the board each survey question as you ask it and the number of students who raise their hands. After the survey, discuss the results. Students may find that they have more similarities than they'd thought — and/or more differences.

HIGH FIVE ..., FOUR ..., THREE ..., TWO ..., ONE ..., ZERO

Ask the students to each hold up the fingers on one hand to give a rating from 0 to 5 that indicates where he or she is on each of the continua that you will be reading. Then, read any of a number of continua, such as the following:

- If "introvert" is 0 and "extrovert" is 5 ....
- If "detailed" is 0 and "big picture" is 5 ....
- If "serious" is 0 and "humorous" is 5 ....
- If "loose cannon" is 0 and "analysis paralysis" is 5 ....
- If "easy with money" is 0 and "frugal" is 5 ....
- If "relaxed" is 0 and "anxious" is 5 ....
- If "live for the moment" is 0 and "plan for the future" is 5 ....

Comment on any general tendencies or on the balance of tendencies, to help the students become more aware of the differences in personalities among them.

BEST COURSES AND BEST INSTRUCTORS

Ask each student to answer the following questions:

- What was the best college course you have ever taken?
- Why was this course the best?
- What qualities make the best instructors?

List the characteristics of the best courses and the best instructors on the board. Develop the results into a short discussion of different ways of learning and different approaches to teaching. Be ready for some comments that show a different understanding of what makes the "best" instructors, e.g., "Professor X was the best because his class met in a bar." If you don't let such comments catch you by surprise, you can probe for the students to explain how they learned better with these "best" instructors.

31. Do a 180 with this activity.

As a follow-up to the discussion, ask each student to mention the qualities that he or she thinks make an instructor "less than the best." List these qualities on the board and encourage the students to discuss them.

How Do You Learn?

Tell the students that you're going to read a list of teaching approaches and techniques and ask them to raise their hands when you read an approach or technique that works well for their learning style. Here are a few to consider including in your list:

- lecture
- discussion
- pictures, diagrams, and graphs
- demonstrations
- working in pairs
- working in small groups
- question-and-answer
- homework assignments
- making presentations

Make sure that you include your usual approaches and techniques. This exercise can help you understand what approaches and techniques might work well with your students, of course. But it can also help your students understand their learning styles — and those who may have thought they were alone in their style can realize that others learn as they do.

Category: Fun Stuff

PURPOSE: to make it easier for your students to get to know each other

The icebreakers in this category are similar to icebreakers used in other social settings. Sure, you're not hosting a mixer, a cocktail party, a gathering of new project volunteers, or a baby shower, but it's important for students to interact as people, not more narrowly in their role as students. Although the title of this category is "Fun Stuff," the purpose is not to entertain, but rather to encourage personal connections.

ORDER WITHOUT WORDS

Announce that the wall at one side of the room is January 1 and the wall at the opposite side is December 31. Then ask the students to line up from one wall to the other in order of their birthdays. The trick here is that they may use gestures only; they must figure out where to stand without saying or writing a word. Then, when the students have finished lining up, have each state his or her birthday, starting from the January 1 wall and going to the December 31 wall. The purpose of this activity is for students to work together as strangers without using words.

32. Conduct an anonymous discussion.

Ask the students to write down their feelings about the activity — how it worked, what they learned, or whatever. Then ask them to pass their papers around the room for a few seconds. Then call "Stop!" and make sure that each has a paper. Have each student read the paper that ended up with him or her and ask the students to comment. Since nobody will know whose comments are being read, the discussion begins anonymously. This exercise provides an interesting study in collaboration under constraints and a follow-up discussion can bring forth some valuable insights.

Nuts and Bolts

Bring to class various sizes of bolt-and-nut combinations — enough for a nut or a bolt for every student. Distribute the nuts and bolts. Then ask the students to each find the student who has a piece of hardware that matches.

33. Go beyond the basic nuts and bolts.

To complicate the exercise, include a washer or two for each bolt, so that students must form groups of three or four.

String Thing

This activity works best with smaller classes. Start by holding a ball of yarn or twine in your throwing hand and the end in your other hand. State your name. Then toss the ball to a student, who is to introduce himself or herself, hold the yarn or twine in one hand, and toss the ball to another student. The students continue to toss the ball until all of them have introduced themselves. Point out that all of them entered your class as individuals and perhaps strangers, but now they have started forming ties as members of a community. Then ask the students to rewind the ball of yarn or twine, by reversing the unwinding. As they try to do so, you can point out that they will leave the class at the end of the term as individuals again, but not quite the same. To save time, you may choose to have the students leave the yarn or string where it is, as a reminder of the ties they're forming and hope that one volunteers to stay after class to rewind the yarn or twine.

34. Add something of interest.

When you give your name, also give an interesting fact about yourself. Then, ask each student to do so. Katy J. Vopal points out that you can establish a pattern to guide the activity, such as one of the following:

- words of wisdom or a quote that you live by
- something that you are an expert on (an area of interest, a hobby, etc.)

- the first thing you would do with a million dollars
- three things you would save if your house or apartment were on fire

WHO AM I?

For each student in your class, write the name of a famous person on an index card. Then, use masking tape to attach a card to each student's back or on their forehead. The students then mingle and each tries to guess who he or she is by asking classmates only yes-or-no questions.

35. Make it relevant.

Rather than use famous names from history, TV, movies, cartoons, music, art, and so forth, choose people who were or are relevant in some way to the course subject. That way, the students have a chance to apply what they know and learn a little.

SIMPLE INTRODUCTION

Call on each student, one by one, to stand and face the other students and give his or her name. Don't follow any obvious order or pattern, so that students are less likely to zone out and not pay attention until it's their turn.

36. Involve your students more fully.

For introductions, the simpler the format, the harder to make it work. Students who are simply giving their names or maybe a little information are likely to treat the activity as routine, of little interest — something to endure. Standing and facing the other students, rather than you, involves them physically, at least minimally. Involve them emotionally as well: ask them to provide information that is not routine. It can be something unrelated to the course, such as to give their hometown or whether they have any pets.

37. Encourage your students to pay attention.

Ask each student to begin by thanking the previous student by name (e.g., "Thank you, Jane Maxwell") before giving his or her own name.

NAME GAME

This is an icebreaker for smaller classes. Ask the first student to give his or her name. Next, ask the second student to name the first student and then give his or her own name. The remaining students do the same, naming in order all of the students before them. The "Name Game" chain links student after student until it reaches the end, at which point the instructor must repeat the names and close by introducing himself or herself.

38. Share the burden through collaboration.

The "Name Game" — classroom version of the children's game, "I'm going on a trip and I'm packing ..." — can put a lot of pressure on each individual student. In essence, each is doing both an introduction and a performance — a memory test — as the other students wait. Some may laugh nervously as a student has difficulty remembering; others may show sympathy or pity. Either way, it can be tough, and make for an unforgettable bad memory among strangers. Here's an easy variant that should cause less pressure: have each student introduce himself or herself in turn; then have the other students name the students in order, finishing the chain with the most recent student. That way, each student does only an introduction and the memory test is a group activity, so there's less pressure.

39. Lessen the pressure by working in groups.

Break the introduction into groups of five to seven students. Although this game is a good way for students to associate names and faces, it works best for those earlier in the chain, whose name-face connection is repeated once for every other student, and less well for those toward the end of the introduction chain, who get far less exposure. If the introductions are in groups of five to seven, there's less disparity between the earlier students and the later students.

40. Reverse the order to better focus the activity.

If you do the Name Game for groups of students, you can add a twist by calling out "Reverse!" so the students must repeat the names of the group members in reverse order. It's more difficult, yes, but it challenges the students to associate the names with individuals rather than people in a sequence.

41. Create labels to make the names more memorable.

Have the students introduce themselves by adding an adjective to their names. Suggest that they choose an alliterative or memorable adjective that characterizes them, such as "Caring Cheryl" or "Bubbling Betsy" or "Sleepy Sam." You may want to offer a few examples to get them thinking, and so the first student has some precedents to follow.

42. Split your head and wear two hats.

Try to learn as many names as possible during this icebreaker, but also think as a facilitator and be attentive to expressions and body language that indicates discomfort or concern. You will have other opportunities to learn your students' names — but never another opportunity to help your students feel welcome in your course.

43. Do the activity now and again.

Repeat this activity at the beginning of the next few classes, varying the order, to help your students learn each other's name — and to warm them up and get them involved.

SHAPES

Make the activity circular. Ask the students to form a circle. Then, have each student give his or her name and make a motion with his or her hand or body. The other students repeat the name and the motion. As each student does his or her introduction, the other students repeat the name and the motion of each of the students to that point, in sequence.

44. Be careful about involving body parts.

Some students may feel awkward about waving their hands or their bodies in front of strangers — especially if the motion causes any laughter. Others may be very theatrical. The feelings experienced in the first moments of the course may embarrass students and even haunt them for a while. Finally, a memorable motion may cause students and the instructor to remember the names of a few members of the class but eclipse the initial presence of others, probably the more introverted members of the class who would naturally have a harder time participating.

45. Do the activity digitally.

For a tamer version of Shapes, ask the students to each give his or her name and then hold up a number of fingers, on one hand or both. Then the other students repeat the name and hold up the number of fingers for each of the students to that point, in sequence.

LIAR, LIAR!

Give each student an index card. Ask them to write three statements about themselves — two true and one false. Then, call on each student to read his or her statements to the other students, who then ask a total of 10 questions in order to determine which statement is false. After the 10 questions, ask the students to vote by raising their hands for the statement they believe to be untrue. This activity encourages creativity and participation.

46. Show the students how to lie.

You can start this icebreaker by being the first to play. This approach not only models the activity but also shows right away that you're willing to get involved in the action, that you're not aloof and distant from your students.

47. Group the students to grill and guess.

Form groups of three to six students. Then allow each group to ask one question, in turn, of any students not in that group.

WHO HERE ...?

Invite each student to stand and ask a question of his or her classmates, concerning their interests, experiences, or wishes related to the course in particular or to the field in general, using the structure, "Who here ...?" For example, "Who here is planning on a career in this field?" or "Who here has had trouble with this subject?" or "Who here would like to take this course pass/fail or for no grade?" or "Who here reads books in this field for fun?" The other students answer in the affirmative by raising a hand.

48. Find out more through follow-up questions.

You can intervene after an answer by asking a follow-up question. Here are some examples. The question "Who here is planning on a career in this field?" could lead naturally to "What do you want to do specifically?" The question "Who here would like to take this course pass/fail or for no grade?" could lead logically to "Why?" The question "Who here reads books in this field for fun?" could lead to "What have you read lately?" or "Which books would you recommend to other students?"

PICK A CARD, ANY CARD

On index cards, at least enough for one card for every two students, write out quotations, one per card. The quotes may be relevant to the course subject, to college or education in general, or philosophical — serious or humorous. (There are abundant Web sites with quotations.) Then have the students pair up, spread the cards as for a card trick (quotations away from the students), and have a student from each pick one of the cards. Tell the students to discuss their quotation for X minutes. (Set an appropriate time, probably between three and eight minutes, based on the subject and tone of the quotations.)

49. Share the wisdom with the whole class.

After the students have discussed their quotations, have each pair of students report their comments and conclusions to the rest of the class.

50. Encourage contributions as collaboration.

Ask your students for quotations that they find interesting, provocative, or even just weird. This shows the students from the start that you're interested in what they can contribute — and that they should consider themselves collaborators in the learning experience.

51. Think of your students in future courses.

Jot down the best quotations contributed by your students, so you can include them when you use this icebreaker again.

52. Get involved more personally.

You can create a few quotations of your own, using a pseudonym, either to inject a little humor or to raise some controversial points.

53. Continue building on the activity throughout the term.

Post a quotation on a classroom wall at regular intervals, maybe twice a week, to encourage the students to think and discuss. You could begin class by asking for comments on the quote, to warm up their minds.

A PENNY FOR YOUR MEMORIES

Put a few carefully selected pennies in a bag. Then ask each student, one by one, to draw a penny from the bag, read the date, and tell the most important or memorable thing that he or she did or was doing that year.

54. Keep it real and relevant for your students.

You may want to focus on more recent memories by excluding pennies more than 20 years old. (How many times do you want to hear, "I wasn't even born yet!"?) Consider the range of ages that you expect among your students. As a variant, you could ask them to cite something that happened that year that would be of interest in the subject area. For example, in a literature course they could name a book that was published or an author who died in that year, in a history or current events course they could mention an event, or in the sciences or mathematics they could cite discoveries or inventions. If a student hesitates, invite the other students to jump in and help, to make it a community activity.

Category: Getting More Personal

PURPOSE: to encourage your students to share and explore
their differences

The icebreakers in this category, as the title indicates, promote interactions that bring out more personal aspects, the individualities among your students. There's a thin line between sharing our personal lives and feeling an invasion of privacy — and it's not the same line for any of us, especially with strangers. These icebreakers should be appropriate, but use them with sensitivity.

PLAYING FAVORITES

Ask each student to name his or her favorite ... whatever. You can choose the category — book, movie, dessert, type of food, possession, etc. — or leave the choice to each student. You may also wish to have them explain why such and such is their favorite.

55. Follow up on the favorites.

Instead of having the students explain their favorites to all of their classmates, group them in twos or threes according to same or similar favorites. Then, ask them to discuss their favorites and their reasons.

56. Mix rather than match your students.

Arrange groups to discuss their favorites — but bring together students whose favorites are very different. This is a good introduction to discussing differences.

57. Select subjects with sensitivity.

Avoid any activity that might oblige any student to reveal any information that he or she considers too personal. That's a tough call. Foods and movies and books, for example, might seem like safe choices, but foods could involve dietary restrictions for people of some religions and movies and books might get into politics, religion, sexuality and sexual orientation, and other areas. What can you do? Always allow any student to pass on his or her turn — without giving any reason. Icebreakers are to make students feel comfortable, not to test them.

DREAM VACATION

Ask each student to introduce himself or herself by name and then to describe, in detail, the dream vacation and explain why it's perfect.

58. Start with volunteers.

Putting students "on the spot" can work against your purposes of making them feel comfortable with you and with each other.

GUESSING GAME

This is an activity for large classes, when there are too many students for any real interaction of significant duration. Tell the students that you're going to mention a few things about yourself and make guesses about how many of them have any of those things in common with you. You'd like them to raise their hands if you're right. Take, for example, an instructor teaching introductory psychology with 100 students. She might begin by saying, "I started studying psychology because I wanted to understand myself better. I'd guess that about 50 of you have the same reason. Hands? Oh, only about 30. I'm not doing very well so far. OK. I'd guess that maybe 75 of you are taking this course because it's required. Hands? OK, at least 60 or 70 — I did better on that one. I was born in Pennsylvania. I'm guessing that there are five of you who were born there too. Hands? I count eight. That's close enough. ...." This activity allows the students and you to get a sense of commonalities — reasons for taking the course, experience in the subject area, and so on — and to have a little fun. The students also learn some things about you in a casual, personal way. Also, because the students are raising their hands and probably twisting around in their seats to count the hands, they're participating physically.

59. Let the students grade you.

Why not let them participate more actively in Guessing Game, by rating your guesses? For each guess, ask for them to raise their hands to indicate a grade. "So, I guessed 50 out of 100 or so and there are 30. How many of you would give me an A on that effort? Hands up. Only five? OK. How about a B? 10 hands? That's better? A C? I count about 25 or 30. Maybe a D? OK, about 50? So, I guess that I fail on that one. So, let's try another ...." By doing a role reversal, you make more of a game out of this activity and bring up the issue of grades — often a source of anxiety — in a way that's casual and even fun.

60. Let the students guess about you.

Neil Singleton, a communications instructor at Indiana State University, uses a guessing game he calls "First Impressions." In the first few minutes of the first class, he asks his students to write down what they think about him; e.g., "You look strict" or "I think you're married" or "I'll bet you're a Pacers fan." He collects the guesses and then reads each one and confirms or corrects it. He's found it to be a fun way to introduce himself and to help the students express concerns, assumptions, fears, and expectations.

MORE LIKE THIS OR LIKE THAT?

Mark two areas of the room, such as opposite sides opposite corners with a pair of contrasting terms — by writing on the board or putting each term on a sheet of flip chart or other paper and taping the sheets to the wall. (See the list of suggestions following these instructions.) Then, ask the students to each go to one of the two areas by choosing between the two terms: "Are you more like ... or like ...?" Next, the students in each area should pair up and discuss their reasons for choosing that area.

Suggested contrasts:

Are you more like ...

- An SUV or a hybrid compact?
- The East Coast or the Midwest?

- A roller skate or a pogo stick?
- A tortoise or a hare?
- An oak or a willow?
- A babbling brook or a quiet lake?
- A cow or a horse?
- A file cabinet or a liquor cabinet?
- A gourmet restaurant or a fast food joint?

61. Take it to the people to bring it all together.

This is a good way for students to pair up and get to know each other. Unfortunately, after the activity, each member of the class knows only one other person — or maybe the two just chatted ... or one dominated the conversation and the other just listened. And what do the students in each pair know about each other? Maybe a lot, maybe very little of substance. So have each member of each pair report back to the other students. This motivates each to take notes and ask questions ... and every student gets to know something about every other student.

62. Get physical and mix it up.

Mark a line down the middle of the room, either with tape or string or virtually, by indicating with your hand a line from some point on one side of the room to some point on the other. Then read a series of either-or statements such as "I like lizards or snakes," "I prefer night or day," "I like hot dogs or hamburgers." The choices in your statements can be serious or silly, general or specific. After you read a statement, students agreeing with the first choice move to one side of the line and students agreeing with the second choice move to the other side of the line; any students who can't decide or who like both equally straddle the line.

WE ALL NEED HEROES

Ask each student to name someone that he or she would consider a hero and give reasons. Our choice of heroes can reveal a lot about us: they embody qualities that we admire, they do things that we would like to emulate. They bring out similarities and differences among students and may generate emotional discussion — so be prepared to keep the activity moving!

63. Make it a meeting.

Put the following sentences on the board or a transparency and ask the students to write down what they would put in the blanks: "If I could meet any person, living or dead, it would be _____ because _____. I would like to talk with this person about _____." Allow three to five minutes, then ask each student to read his or her choice, reasons, and topics to the class.

WHAT I LIKE ABOUT ME

Ask each student to give his or her name and mention one thing that he or she really likes about himself or herself.

64. Ease into the ego thing.

Ask for volunteers first. Then, choose students who seem more extroverted or at least less hesitant than the others. As more students introduce themselves, this activity should feel less risky for the remaining students.

THREE WISHES

Ask each student to name three things that he or she would change if a genie in a bottle gave him or her three wishes — and the reasons for choosing these three things.

WHAT'S IN A NAME?

Ask the students to each describe how or why he or she received his or her name. Some may have been named after a grandfather or grandmother, an uncle or an aunt. Some may have been named after a place. Some may have been given a name picked from a book or a name that "just sounded right."

65. Give students a chance to shine, if possible — but just don't expect it.

Names and their origins can be very interesting — but sometimes a name is, well, just a name. For example, a student may have a distinctive name that reveals a fascinating story about several generations of the family. The next student may be only able to say, "My name is John ... and I don't know why." If that's their first connection with the other students, it may be embarrassing. Also, some students may feel uncomfortable explaining their unusual names or perhaps not knowing the reason behind the names. So, the answer to the question that Shakespeare posed in *Romeo and Juliet*, "What's in a name?" may be, as Juliet believed, nothing: "That which we call a rose by any other name would smell as sweet." You could offer your students two alternatives: "If you were to change your name, what name would you choose and why?" and "If you have any children, what are/will be their names and why?"

ADJECTIVES

Have each student introduce himself or herself using seven adjectives and then explain why he or she chose each adjective. Allow the students at least two minutes to think and to write down their adjectives and reasons.

66. Put a spin on it.

Have your students use nouns instead of adjectives. Or, more interesting, use verbs.

67. Choose icebreakers that can be scaled up or down easily.

You should be able to adjust the activity according to the number of students and/or the amount of time available. For the activity above, the number of adjectives can be raised or lowered and it works just as well.

68. Focus on your goals, not the rules.

If, in this example, there are students who use nouns instead of adjectives, it doesn't matter: the goal is to get the students to introduce themselves in an unusual way. Whether they use adjectives or nouns or adverbs or other parts of speech, the other students are getting to know something about them.

69. Do it yourself.

Explain how the activity works — and then introduce yourself with seven adjectives. How well does it work for you? How do you feel doing it? Then remember that the students will have only two minutes to choose their adjectives and that each will be doing the introduction in front of dozens of strangers. Will any feel uncomfortable doing this ice-breaker intended to make them feel more comfortable?

SOMEONE SIMILAR IN TWO WAYS

Have students each write two adjectives describing themselves on a stick-on name tag. Then, ask them to each find someone with similar adjectives. The two should then talk for a few minutes about why they each chose those two adjectives.

70. Try it with opposites.

Have each student find someone with opposite adjectives. As in "Someone Similar in Two Ways," the two should then talk for a few minutes about why they each chose those two adjectives.

71. Talk about words.

Have the partners of each pair introduce each other to their classmates — and then explain why they consider the adjectives to be opposites. Invite the other students to offer their opinions. This is a good way to get students thinking about their use of words and their denotations and connotations, which can be good preparation if you intend to involve your students in discussions.

72. Decrease the complexity in order to increase interactions.

Have the students use only one adjective. Allow them three minutes to meet another person with a similar adjective and discuss their commonality. Then, have them move on to find another and discuss. Depending on the time available, you could have each student meet two to five or six others. Beyond that number, it may become difficult to keep them all separate. Suggest that the students keep notes of the names and anything else that might help them remember the classmates they meet.

Happy Birthday to Us

Have each student find the student whose birthday (month and date, not year) is the closest to his or hers. The two should then find at least two things that they have in common.

73. Share the pairs with the other students.

Have the partners of each pair introduce each other to their classmates — names, birthdays, and the things the two have in common.

Scavenger Hunt

Give each student an index card with three to 10 items on it, such as "favorite color is yellow" or "likes liver" or "collects coins." The students must find a student who matches each of the items and write his or her name beside that item. The first person to match all of his or her items to students wins the game.

74. Make the items relevant to college life and/or the subject matter.

It might make students feel less uncomfortable than if they were learning about each other's personal life.

75. Make the items connect students personally.

Use statements such as "Find someone who is interested in the same hobby as you," "Find someone who was born in the same year as you," "Find someone who was born in the same month as you," "Find someone who was born in the same state as you," or "Find someone who drives the same model of car as you."

76. Share the connections ... and the gaps.

If you use items that connect students personally, have the students with the five most matches and the students with the five fewest matches tell the class the traits that they matched ... or failed to match. You can also ask each person who matches (whether the winning students found them or not) to introduce himself or herself by name. This way at least 10 students introduce themselves by name and a few facts and most or all of the others introduce themselves by name, within the context of a game.

CIRCLES

Give each student a sheet of paper with a circle in the middle surrounded by smaller circles. Ask them to write their name in the middle circle and the names of groups with which they identify in the other circles (e.g., age group, groups to which they belong, favorite sports teams, etc.). Then ask them to find three other students in the class who have the same groups in their smaller circles.

77. Be aware of too much of a good thing.

This exercise can be great in an introductory course or any other course in which the students may be particularly anxious and come from diverse backgrounds. When they group by interests and affiliations, individuals will feel a better sense of belonging. However, in a course in which the students will be discussing hot issues (such as politics, religion, economics, or sociology), it's important not to emphasize any common areas that may tend to divide and polarize students.

BINGO

Give each student a bingo card — a sheet of paper with a five-by-five matrix, each square containing an item such as the following:

- is an only child
- keeps a journal or a diary
- enjoys camping
- is left-handed
- enjoys biking
- enjoys hiking
- enjoys classical music
- skis (snow or water)
- skates (ice, inline, or roller)
- takes naps
- plays a musical instrument

- is interested in genealogy
- has visited the Grand Canyon
- has visited Disneyworld
- has traveled somewhere in Europe
- speaks French
- is a marketing major

Tell the students that they are to move around the room and find other students who match the squares on their bingo sheet. When they find a match, that student should sign the matrix square corresponding to the matching item.

78. Consider adding rules to ensure more mingling.

Some (many? most?) will realize that they can just interrogate each student item by item and find as many matches as possible with each, so they can fill their cards with the fewest face-to-face interactions and in minimal time. Since the purpose of this activity is for each student to meet as many others as possible, not to fill the cards as quickly as possible, that method defeats the purpose of the activity. So, you may want to limit the number of times a student can sign any one sheet.

79. Avoid items that might be too personal.

Risky topics would generally include politics, religion, and sex. Also, some students may be embarrassed to admit that they take naps, for example, or that they collect Barbie dolls or Star Wars action figures.

80. Ease up a little to shorten the time required for an icebreaker.

In this example, you could add one or two or three wild (blank) squares to each card, in the center and in one corner or two opposite corners, so the students have to fill only four or even three squares in a row to win.

81. Adjust to your environment.

This icebreaker is one that's sometimes called a milling exercise, because students should be able to move around the room easily to interact. That could be difficult in a room that's small or if the desks or chairs cannot be moved, as in an auditorium. If that's the situation, modify.

In this example, the rules could be changed. You could prepare cards on which there are different traits among the squares and/or the squares are arranged differently. Then, have each student in turn read out a square on his or her card. Or, you could make a list of all the descriptions and then read them off one by one, in any order. Either way, you would ask any students who fit the description to raise their hands and call out their names. There are disadvantages with this modification: the exercise would be noisier, maybe even chaotic, and there's no one-to-one interaction.

82. Remember that some students may have mobility problems.

If you plan a milling exercise, make sure that there's ample room for all students to move around freely and easily.

83. Make it relevant to the course.

In this example, instead of using descriptions that are generic, compose descriptions that relate to the subject matter. Here are a few examples: in a math or engineering course, "knows someone who owns a slide rule," or in a French course, "has visited Quebec," or in a biology course, "has eaten insects."

MAKING CHANGES

Group your students into pairs. The students in each pair must stand facing each other. Tell them to look at their partners closely. Then have them turn away from their partners. Tell them that you will count to 20 and that, during that time, each of them is to change five things about his or her appearance. For example, they might remove their glasses, switch their watch from one wrist to another, untie a shoelace, remove a shoe, put on lipstick, or undo a shirt button. Then, when you reach 20, have the partners turn around and face each other again. Each student must then identify the five changes in his or her partner.

84. Be attentive to discomfort.

With students who are less outgoing, this exercise may be more difficult. When a student might prefer to be just another face in the crowd, an exercise that requires students to scrutinize each other may make him or her uncomfortable. Also, students from some cultures might naturally avoid eye contact. You should mention that no student is required to participate. If any students are participating but having problems, you might gesture to them or whisper suggestions to them for changes they could make, to make it easier to participate.

INTERVIEWS

Have the students form pairs and then have each partner interview the other for two minutes. (You may want to suggest some questions to start the activity with or post a list on the board or an overhead.) Then, bring the pairs back together and have each student introduce his or her partner to the rest of the students by giving them information gained in the interview.

Some suggestions for interviewing:

- If you could travel anywhere in the world, where would you go? Why?
- What would you be doing right now if you weren't here in this class?
- What color best expresses your personality? Why?
- What would you buy if you had the money? Why?
- Who do you consider the most important person in the world at this moment? Why?

85. Keep it short and interesting.

The interview should provide just some glimpses into the students. Two minutes should be enough for each introduction, with a minute for each student. If the class is too large for the time available, give a single question and allow 30 seconds for each interview.

86. Try another perspective.

Ask the students to introduce themselves from the perspective of their best friend or their pet. That perspective may allow them a certain distance that may make it more comfortable for some students to talk about themselves.

CARD A CLASSMATE

Give each student a blank index card and ask them to each write three statements about himself or herself: e.g., an interest, a hobby, favorite things — outdoor activity, movie, book, color, vacation spot, or whatever. They give the cards to you, you shuffle them, and then you hand one to each student, asking that any student who receives his or her card return it to you. Each student then tries to find the person whose card he or she holds. As they succeed, the found student introduces himself or herself to the class, giving his or her name and the information on the card.

87. Select the items to be included.

It may be appropriate to specify certain items to be included. For example, if you teach geography, you might select birthplace and favorite vacation spot, or if you teach literature, you might select favorite book and least favorite book. You could then ask follow-up questions, such as "Why is that your favorite vacation spot?" or "Why do you like that book least?"

THREE SPECIAL PEOPLE

Have each student give his or her name, identify three people who have helped him or her develop and reach this point, and then explain how each person helped. You should model the activity by going first.

88. Make it theatrical.

Set the stage for your students by wording your introduction as an acceptance speech, e.g., "My name is Nicole Lauren and I would like to thank three people for helping me get this far ...." Emphasize that this activity is not about being on stage but about expressing appreciation for some important people in your life.

TOUGH QUESTIONS!

Print out the following questions — and/or questions that you create — on slips of paper. Then tell your students that they will each be drawing a question to answer. Tell them that you will allow each of them about two minutes to answer and that anyone who does not feel comfortable answering the question can pass and draw another question.

Some tough questions:

- What is the best book you have ever read? Why?
- What is the best movie you have ever seen? Why?
- What comes to mind first when you hear the word "reality"? Why?
- Who is the most powerful person in our time? Why?
- What is your favorite sport? Why?
- What color best expresses your personality? Why?
- Whom do you consider the most important person in the world at this moment? Why?
- If you could travel anywhere in the world, where would you go? Why?
- What is the most beautiful thing about people? Why?
- What is the ugliest thing you know? Why?
- What do you like to do most with a free hour? Why?
- What is the most significant event of the last three months? Why?
- What are the most important qualities for a friend? Why?
- What is the most overwhelming thing you know? Why?
- What is the greatest problem in the United States? Why?
- If you could choose to be an animal, what animal would you choose? Why?
- What is the greatest crime one person can commit against another? Why?
- What do you feel when you stand on the shore of the ocean?
- What word would best describe your life up to this moment? Why?
- What institution is most in need of change? Why?
- What one word would you choose to describe a sunset? Why?
- What TV advertisement bothers you the most? Why?
- What is the biggest waste, in your opinion? Why?
- What will you be doing 10 years from now?

- What will save American politics? Why?
- What future discovery do you anticipate the most? Why?
- What is the greatest music ever composed? Why?

89. Reverse roles to share responsibilities.

Ask the students to suggest tough questions for you to answer. A role reversal sends the message that you expect your students to be collaborating with you in creating a good learning environment — and that they should feel free to ask you questions. Jot down the questions they ask. It shows that you appreciate their contributions. Also, you can include the better ones when you use this icebreaker again.

Category: Going Collaborative

PURPOSE: to establish an active, participatory environment by getting the students working together, in pairs or small groups

Many instructors have their students work collaboratively; in fact, that skill may be the most important as the students enter into careers. If you intend to have your students work together in groups, you may want to use an icebreaker from this section to encourage teamwork from the start. If you are assigning group projects in your course, Katy J. Vopal suggests using one of these icebreakers just before your students start their projects. (She also recommends mixing personality types in the groups.)

KNOTS

Divide the students into teams of eight to 12. Have the students in each group form a circle and place their hands out in the middle. Have each student join his or her right hand with the hand of another member of the group, but neither student standing immediately to the left or the right. Have each student do the same with his or her left hand. Then, ask the students in each group to get untangled without letting go of the hands they're holding. They may loosen their holds to be able to twist and turn, but they must remain attached. They may step over or under other members of the group. The first group to untangle their knot wins.

There are four possible solutions to the knot:

1. One large circle with students facing in either direction

2. Two interlocking circles

3. A figure eight

4. A circle within a circle

It's possible, although improbable, that students will be unable to untangle their knot or to end in two separate circles.

90. Imagine the results — and check against your purposes.

An icebreaker could be a lot of fun, but how do the students benefit from joining hands and then untangling? Maybe a sense of chaotic teamwork. If that's important to your course, great! But you should have good reasons for choosing this icebreaker or any other. As mentioned earlier, creativity counts, but only if it makes an icebreaker more effective. Your general purpose for using an icebreaker should be to make the students feel more comfortable.

91. Anticipate personal and cultural sensitivities.

Some people are uncomfortable touching strangers — even shaking hands. How will they feel to be gripping hands and then rubbing bodies as they undo the knots? Such an invasion of their comfort zone may not help them start the course off well.

92. Form groups yourself; don't leave it to the students.

For some icebreakers, students form groups by choosing other students. It's generally best to avoid this method of grouping because of the pressure it can place on students and the stress it can cause. For some, it may bring back high school memories of choosing teams in gym class or pairing up at dances — memories very painful for some students. Also, it's generally faster if you form the groups than if you ask the students to do it.

93. Scramble your students.

It's tempting to group students according to where they're sitting. However, in many classes, that means pulling together students who already know each other. It might be more beneficial to pick a pattern that will scramble the students, such as grouping the students who are first in every other row, the students who are first in the remaining rows, the students who are second in every other row, and so forth.

BRAIN STRAIN

Divide the students into groups of three or four. Give each group a sheet of paper and a pencil. Have each group write out answers to three to five questions that you put on the board or a transparency. The first group to turn in its paper to you with all correct answers wins.

Here are some sample questions:

- What is the largest lake in North America?
- What are the names of the planets, in order, starting from the sun?
- What is the national language of Brazil?
- Which U.S. president was killed within a week after the Civil War ended?
- What eight states begin with M?
- What scientist developed the Theory of Relativity?
- Name the six most recent presidents.
- What is the full name of the author of the book *Moby Dick*?
- What is the capital of Canada?
- Who developed the theory of evolution?
- Who wrote the play *A Midsummer Night's Dream*?
- What is the name of the decoration given to members of the U.S. armed forces who are wounded in action against an enemy?

94. Keep it nice and light and easy.

Icebreakers are intended to help students feel more comfortable around each other and you; anything that seems like a quiz or a mental competition is likely to raise the anxiety level of at least some students. Think of the game of Trivial Pursuit®. The name indicates that it's about trivia, but the way that some players take it so seriously, it's anything but trivial. So, keep the questions enjoyable, even funny.

STRANDED

Form teams of four or five students. Tell them that each group is stranded on an island. The members of each group are to list the five things that they should have brought on their trip in case of a shipwreck. Allow five minutes for the groups to discuss the possibilities and develop their lists. Then, have each group report on its list. Write on the board the items listed by each group. Then, have the students compare and discuss the relative merits of each choice.

95. Make it more difficult with a little variation.

Ask the groups to identify five people whom they would want with them if they were stranded on an island. Each group then reports to the class and gives its reasons for choosing those five people.

GROUP PROJECT

Break the class into groups of four to six students. Give each group an assignment appropriate to the course subject, such as a problem to solve or a topic for discussion that will generate an answer, a list, or some other result. For example, a biology 101 instructor could ask the groups to define such terms as metabolism, oxidation, photosynthesis, ionization, and homeostasis, or to identify such people as Aristotle, Carl Linnaeus, Gregor Mendel, and Charles Darwin and their contributions to biology. Another example: An American history instructor could ask the groups to generate a list of the 10 most significant events of the 20th century or five major events from the 1960s. After 10 or 15 minutes, have each group report back to the rest of the students on its results.

96. Start on the first assignment.

If you have a homework assignment scheduled for the first class, consider giving the groups five minutes or so to start working on it. This introduces the students to working together and it helps ease them into their first assignment from you.

97. Study the syllabus.

An alternative to having the groups start on an assignment is to hand out the course syllabus and ask the groups to find the answers to a series of questions about the syllabus that you then put on the board, an overhead, or other display. Most instructors know from experience that their students typically ask certain questions during the term for which they could find the answers if they read the syllabus again. After allowing sufficient time for the groups to find the answers, ask the questions of the class. Close the activity by asking if any of the students have any questions of their own that the syllabus doesn't answer. Answer them — and make a note to revise the syllabus for the next time around.

THE TRUTH IS OUT THERE

Divide the students into groups of two, three, or four, depending on the number in your class and the type and number of activity items that you prepare. Then, give each group one item and ask the question, "How would you find out ...?" The items that you give the groups should be factual research questions appropriate to the subject matter of your course and the level, more or less. For example, in history the items might be people or places or dates. In architecture, you could ask about the construction materials or dimensions of buildings or you could name structures and ask about the architects and when the structures were built. In sociology, the items might be about theories and the people behind them. Even if the facts seem trivial within the context of your course, the purpose is to challenge your students to collaborate. After allowing enough time for the students to identify possible sources, discuss them, and decide on the best, ask each group to present to the class its item and the source(s) the members have chosen. Encourage the other students to comment and perhaps suggest other sources, so that the entire class is collaborating.

98. Push for the truth.

You can emphasize that students should always be questioning information that they obtain from any source, even directly. This is especially true as more of us are getting information from the Web. You can add a second question to this activity: "How would you verify the information that you got from your first source?" Depending on the subject of the course, you might ask the groups to decide on a third source.

99. Learn from comparative collaboration.

You could give several groups the same item, if the groups are located far enough apart in the room. Then, when the groups present their sources, you can compare the sources they've chosen.

Category: Dealing with Feelings

PURPOSE: to bring out students' feelings about the subject and the course, to lead students into the course, to generate interest

Instructors are generally focused on the mind, not the emotions, but we all recognize that it's a package deal: our students feel as well as think — and often their feelings get in the way of their thinking. If you suspect that your students might have anxieties beyond the usual butterflies of starting a course, if you're concerned that there may be emotions that might make it harder to develop a sense of community and might impede their learning, consider the icebreakers in this section.

I'M IN THIS CLASS BECAUSE ....

Go around the room and have each student give his or her name and complete this sentence: "I am in this class because ...."

100. Establish common ground.

Pass out an index card to each student and ask them to complete the sentence "I am in this class because ...." Then, have each student stand and read his card and hand it to you. Ask students who have the same reason (whether or not they wrote it on their cards) to raise their hand. Tape the card to the board and write down the number of "votes" for that reason. The students will quickly see what they have in common. There may be a lot of students who are taking the course only because it's required or because it fit their schedule. You can accept this reality and assure them that you hope that they'll have many more reasons by the end of the course. It's always good to know how you stand before the course begins! You might want to follow up any "It's required" and

"It fit" answers by asking what they expect to get out of your course — in addition to a grade.

GREAT EXPECTATIONS

Pass out index cards to your students, one to each. Then, leave small piles around the room where they can easily take more as needed. Ask them to write down the expectations that they have for the course and for you. (They should not put their names on the cards.) As they finish, collect the cards. Shuffle them, then read the expectations and comment on each. This is a good way for your students to know how they fit in with their classmates in terms of their expectations — and, of course, for you to know what your students expect.

101. Eliminate the impossible.

You may want to advise your students to post expectations that are realistic. But do so with a sense of humor: "You might want to list 'I expect an A for doing nothing at all' or 'I expect free snacks for every class' — but it's just not going to happen. OK?"

102. Treat each expectation seriously, but honestly.

Show that you're open to their input, but don't make promises that you can't keep and shouldn't even make. If an expectation doesn't seem realistic, say so — tactfully. If an expectation makes sense, tell them.

103. Get your students to walk the talk.

Instead of collecting the cards, have the students come up and tape their cards to the board with masking tape. It may seem like a minor variation, but the physical and psychological involvement of that walk to the front of the room can affect how students feel about your course and participating. It may take a little of the edge off the anxiety for at least some of them. And if they pause for a moment to read some of the other cards, that's good: they're showing an interest in each other from the start.

EXPECTATIONS AND ASSUMPTIONS

Ask the students to each write down five behaviors, attitudes, or qualities that they think you expect of them in your course and five behaviors, attitudes, or qualities that they expect of you. Collect the papers. Then read and list the behaviors, attitudes, or qualities on the board in two columns. If an item is mentioned more than once, place a check mark next to the item for each subsequent mention. Encourage the students to react to the items. How realistic are the items? How do the items interrelate?

104. Keep the results for future classes.

Ask a student to write down the items as you list them on the board. Keep the lists and display them on a transparency or the board periodically throughout the course, to check on how well they and you are meeting their expectations.

DIFFICULTIES AND ISSUES

Ask students to volunteer any difficulties they expect to encounter in the course and any content issues they hope to address. Conduct an open discussion of these difficulties and issues.

105. Focus on issues, not individuals.

A big plus with this exercise is that the instructor and the students focus on difficulties and issues, rather than on the individual students expressing them. The anonymity of this approach allows the students to express concerns that they might hesitate to address if they had to stand and deliver them before a group of strangers. Boarding the contributions fosters a sense of community, of shared concerns from the start.

106. Put the activity on paper.

Have the students write down their difficulties and issues and then turn in their lists. Then list their difficulties and issues on the board, a transparency, or a flip chart. When you've completed the list, conduct an open discussion of the difficulties and issues.

107. Build on positive feelings.

Throughout the term, if you want to ask your students to provide any input on such things as tests, grades, or the difficulty of readings or other assignments — input that could be negative — it may help your students feel more comfortable if you use the "secret vote" approach used in this icebreaker. It would be great if they all felt enough at ease to criticize you or anything about the course — but in the real world, what matters more is to get their input. This approach makes that easier on them.

HOW ARE YOU FEELING?

Ask the students to write down words or phrases that describe how they're feeling about starting the course. Ask them to share their reactions. List them on the board. Then ask them to write down what they think you are feeling at this moment. Ask them to share their thoughts. List them on the board alongside the first list. Invite the students to note any similarities.

108. Encourage and support – don't pressure.

Call on students who volunteer. Don't make anybody participate in sharing or discussing. Since the objective of this activity is to encourage students to feel comfortable in class, forcing them to express their feelings would work against you.

109. Bridge from feelings to responsibilities.

Note the feelings listed on the board and encourage the students to discuss the responsibilities that they have as students and that you have as instructor.

110. Take advantage of anonymity.

Instead of asking the students to share the reactions and thoughts they've each listed, collect their papers. Some students may feel uncomfortable sharing their feelings with strangers. This variation allows them to do so anonymously.

111. Add a little distance for greater comfort.

Change the question from "How are you feeling?" to "How do you think the students around you are feeling?" Some students will project their own feelings; that's good, because it will get those feelings on the board, out in the open. Others will imagine the students around them to be confident, eager to begin; that's good too, because as you conduct the discussion of those positive feelings, you can raise a key question — "Why not you, too? What's keeping any of you from feeling confident and eager?"

By the End of This Course ....

Write on the board, "By the end of this course ...." Ask the students to write out that phrase on a sheet of paper. Then ask them to each finish the sentence to express his or her thoughts and feelings. After a few minutes, ask them to each read his or her sentence to the class. Discuss each completion in terms of a goal and strategies for achieving it. First, ask the student for his or her ideas on strategies. Then, open up the discussion to the class for contributions.

112. Seek similarities.

Record each completion on the board. Then, after all of the students have read their endings to the class, try to group the contributions and discuss them in terms of common goals and strategies for achieving them.

113. Conserve the contributions for closure at the end of the term.

Suggest that the students save their sheets or turn them in to you so you can save either a copy or the original. Then, in the final class, each student can read his or her completion to the class and comment on whether the course turned out as he or she had anticipated and how the strategies had worked or not.

Think Small

Do a mini lesson, a 10-minute version of a typical class, to show how you intend to teach the course. But do it on a topic that is unrelated to the course, perhaps something light, even humorous. (If you have an interesting hobby or enjoy an unusual sport, it might be a good subject.) That way the students don't feel like you're jumping right into the course immediately.

114. Build a bridge to your course.

Do a mini lesson as you would teach the final class of a course that prepares students for your course. In other words, help transition your students by covering what they should have learned most recently (either the preceding term or in high school), but as if it were new, not as a review.

TEACHER AND STUDENT

Group the students into twos or threes. One student in each group will role-play the teacher; the other(s) will role-play the student(s). Tell the "teachers" to teach a lesson, which you designate — something that they should have learned in a previous course. Tell the "students" to be bad — inattentive, asking strange questions, unable to answer questions, and so forth. After about five minutes, have the students switch roles. This can be a fun way for students to get to know each other — and to better understand what you may have to experience in teaching. Bring the pairs together and have the students discuss the inappropriate behaviors and how the "instructors" felt about them and reacted to them.

115. Go from understanding to managing.

Ask the students to suggest ways in which an instructor could deal with the inappropriate student behaviors. Write each behavior on the board and each suggestion for dealing with it.

Category: No Student Is an Island

PURPOSE: to encourage students to be interested in each other, to share information and resources, and to identify their individual needs and goals

One of the concerns expressed by many instructors is that students don't seem interested in each other as part of the educational system. For example, they may take copious notes when the instructor is talking, then stop when a fellow student asks a question or makes a comment. Sometimes it may be because they assume that no contribution from a student will be on the test (and usually they're right in that assumption). But sometimes the cause is deeper: they believe that there is only one source of knowledge in the classroom — you. If you're concerned about that prevalent attitude, maybe one of the icebreakers in this section can help you effect some attitude adjustment from the start.

LEARNING FROM LIFE

Ask each student to tell the others about one interesting and/or valuable thing that he or she has learned in the past week outside of the classroom. This activity can help students think about learning as a 24/7 experience and remind them that they can learn from each other, so that each will appreciate the experience and knowledge of the other students, which will encourage them to be interested in each other's questions and contributions and participate more fully in discussions.

116. Leave the role of instructor.

React to what each student says as you would react to a colleague. Let the other students react first, but then express how you feel. As Katy J. Vopal commented in reviewing the icebreakers in this section, "I even tell the students that I learn from them — and that shocks them. I want them to all feel that their viewpoints, observations, etc. are valuable. And they are! I get new perspectives on the subject material every semester." When you react to your students as people who have much to contribute to the learning community, you are fostering confidence and encouraging collaboration.

What I've Done That's Unique Here

Have each student introduce himself or herself and then state something that he or she has done that perhaps no other student in the class has done. If other students have done that thing, the student must try again, until he or she finds something that makes him or her unique among the other students.

117. Avoid competition.

It may be OK for students to try to one-up each other. However, it may also cause students who feel insecure being in the course to feel even more threatened by other students, knowing for sure — instead of merely imagining — that others have done things that have better prepared them for the course.

118. Expand the activity to share experiences.

You can go beyond the simple unique-or-not focus of this activity by asking each student who comes up with a unique experience to talk about it a little, to share that experience and his or her feelings, what he or she felt, or whatever might be of interest to the other students.

119. Twist the activity to focus on the future.

A variant is to have each student mention something that he or she would really like to do. Then, ask any other students who have done that thing or something similar to identify themselves and describe the experience and their feelings.

Why Am I Here?

Have the students introduce themselves, one by one, and tell why they are there. It may be wise to phrase the question not as "Why are you here?" — especially if the course is required — but rather as "What do you expect to learn in this course?"

120. Get them up standing.

Don't let your students sit unless you're all seated in a circle. Have each student stand and face the others, not you. Make sure that all of the other students can hear and see their classmate; encourage each individual connection. If each student stands, he or she is more likely to commit to the introduction, rather than give a quick, half-audible "My name is ..." and sit down again immediately to blend back into the crowd.

121. Broaden the scope of interest.

You could ask the students to provide some more information, such as explaining why they are interested in the course subject and what they hope to do and learn in the course. This latter question could provide some interesting answers, and might challenge you in terms of how you've planned the course.

Category: Distance Learning

PURPOSE: to foster comfort and confidence in a virtual community

There's no need to explain the purposes of the icebreakers in this final section. If you're not face to face with your students, the icebreakers here are for you — and you probably need them more than your colleagues who teach in conventional settings. It can be difficult to promote a sense of community in an online learning environment. It's also more difficult to choose and use icebreakers in a virtual class, but the benefits can make it well worth the effort.

Icebreakers can help you promote these characteristics of a good online learning community:

- Participants post regularly.
- The online community meets its members' needs, and participants express honest opinions.
- Participant-to-participant collaboration and learning are evident, and spontaneous moderating occurs among the participants.
- Reasonable venting about technology, content, and even the facilitator is acceptable and evident.
- Participants show concern and support for the community. (George Collison, Bonnie Elbaum, Sarah Haavind, and Robert Tinker, *Facilitating Online Learning: Effective Strategies for Moderators*, p. 77)

Movie Star

Film a short introduction (three minutes or so) to yourself and the course. Provide some personal and professional background and briefly describe the benefits of the course for the students, to accompany your written introduction of yourself and the course.

122. Accentuate and facilitate contact.

List all means by which your students can contact you: phone number, e-mail address, fax number. Give your office hours. (By the way, are you holding office hours online as well as in person? If not, why not?)

Read and Reply

Send your students a welcome letter in advance of the first class. Introduce yourself and provide any information they'll need to access course materials. Then, require an e-mail reply within 24 hours or 48 hours to verify that they've received and read your letter.

123. Establish terms of address.

Tell your students how you want them to address you — e.g., "Please call me Jim" or "I'd like you to call me Professor Smith" or "Call me Mary Jane or Ms. Lane, as you prefer." Then — and this is important — ask them how they would like to be addressed. Keep track of their preferences — and address each student as he or she prefers. That shows your students from the beginning that you are going to treat each of them as an individual and respect them as people.

124. Explain the technology.

Give step-by-step instructions for using the technology. Make sure that they know how to participate fully in your course. Don't assume that your students know anything about the technology or the procedures. Explain it all as you would like others to explain technical matters to you — clearly and carefully, in terms that make sense, without being condescending. Provide contact information for any technical support available. Finally, but perhaps most important, reassure them that they can use the technology and succeed in your course.

125. Communicate your expectations and any rules.

Keep in mind what Donald E. Hanna, Michelle Glowacki-Dudka, and Simone Conceição-Runlee advise in *147 Practical Tips for Teaching Online Groups* (Atwood Publishing, 2000, p. 53): "Interactive online courses depend on the relationships and trust developed between and among you and the learners. If the learners are to play an active role in developing the course atmosphere, you must *preliminarily* define the structure, rules, norms, and procedures for course discussions upfront — but then give your learners the chance to suggest important modifications."

126. Encourage your students to visit your Web site.

Give your students the URL for your class Web site and/or your bio blurb, whether on the class Web site or on your faculty page on your institution's Web site. (If you don't have more than the basics on your faculty page, why not? What message does it send to your students when you are not a real virtual presence, when you're doing only the minimum?)

127. Include inquiries.

Use this icebreaker as more than just a way to welcome your students and make sure they can connect with you. Ask a few questions. For example, "Where are you from?" and "How long has it been since you took a course in ...?" Keep it simple and factual; the purpose is primarily for each student to establish contact with you and introduce himself or herself.

128. Build on the beginning.

Require regular e-mails from your students. Every few classes or every week, e-mail them one or more quick questions and require a reply within 24 or 48 hours. Avoid yes-no questions. For example, "What was the most surprising thing that you've learned this week?" or "What information in the last lesson do you consider most useful?" or "Give three questions that you would put on a quiz to cover the last lesson."

129. Comment specifically and productively.

When you comment on what students write, try to do so specifically. A general comment such as "Well put" or "Interesting" helps a student less than a comment that focuses on part of a contribution (e.g., "I find it interesting that you use the term X in regard to ...") or asks a follow-up question (e.g., "And how would you try to determine whether your interpretation is justified?"). In short, work with student comments rather than just acknowledging them with a brief reaction that smacks of a grade.

130. Keep it short.

When you post announcements or write e-mails, be sensitive to length and tone. In a conventional classroom, you might occasionally be a little verbose: a few seconds too much here and there is no big deal, not likely to overwhelm or bore your students — who probably are so accustomed to teachers who talk too much! But a similar overage in a written text is likely to have a greater effect. Break up chunks of texts into short paragraphs, to make them easier to read. (This tip, for example, is too long for a single paragraph: I would break it into two paragraphs.)

131. Make your words work smarter.

You're probably aware that words on a screen, without a face and a body, are less likely to be interpreted as you'd expect than if they were accompanied by an expression and body language. Dr. Albert Mehrabian, a psychologist at UCLA, conducted research on communication and found that words express only 7% of our message, while voice tone conveys 38% and body language (including facial expressions and gestures) conveys 55%. So, before you send e-mails or announcements, read them carefully — again and again — as if you were a student. Are you conveying everything that you want to convey and nothing else?

Here's a reminder from Katy J. Vopal: "Watch spelling, punctuation, etc. If you send students a sloppy e-mail, it can kill your credibility — and it is even more embarrassing if they correct you." But if that happens, think of the correction as an opportunity for you to model how to accept corrections.

132. Be careful whenever you write.

Anything that you write in an e-mail or post in a forum should be something that would not make anybody feel uncomfortable if it were made public. Words can travel and they can endure.

AUTOBIOGRAPHIES

Create a class Web page. Ask each student to e-mail you an autobiography for you to post to the class page. Provide some guidelines: such as 150-200 words, covering home town and state (and country, if from outside the United States), major, interests, and so on. Don't ask for any information that students might consider too personal. Remind them that any student who considers a topic too personal can omit that topic in his or her autobiography. Emphasize that the purpose is to serve as an introduction for the other students and for you.

133. Use photos.

A picture is worth a thousand words. Ask each student to e-mail a digital photo of himself or herself, for you to post to the class page next to the autobiography of that student.

134. Put it in quotes.

Ask each student to e-mail a favorite quote that he or she likes, for you to post to the class page after the autobiography of that student. They can choose their quotes for whatever reasons, from any sources — books, magazines, songs, blogs, bumper stickers, poetry, etc. The only requirement is for the quote to mean something to the student.

135. Encourage your students to provide resources.

Ask them to post URLs for resources and news articles relevant to the course. Then, remind them to do so periodically throughout the course.

136. Encourage personality.

Ask the students to each post a URL that they consider interesting or useful or fun — and that has no connection to the course or the subject matter.

HANGOUT

Create an area online for students to gather casually. It should be a place for them to ask questions of each other or simply to chat. Post on the site any regulations or policies that your institution has established for use of its computer system, and then allow your students total freedom within those limits. They should know that this is their place, just as they might hang out in the student union, a coffee shop, a favorite restaurant, or a bar.

137. Drop in for a visit from time to time.

Be casual ... and be a person, not their instructor. You might, for example, ask if anyone has checked out the new exhibit at the art museum or has seen a certain movie or is following a TV show. Don't try to be a student; just be yourself.

PERSONAL PAGES

Set up a Web page where students can create personal pages. Suggest that they post a photo or several of themselves, describe their lives, list their interests and hobbies — whatever they want to do, within the limits of any regulations or policies that your institution has established for use of its computer system. Some may not want to post pictures of themselves. Ask them to post something that represents them in some way, such as a graphic, a cartoon, a quote that they like, a line of poetry, a picture of a famous person, or a painting. Some may do little or nothing; others may go wild. Whether at either extreme or in-between, it's OK: these are their pages. Many students already have personal pages; encourage them to link to their pages, if they feel comfortable sharing them.

138. Create a page for yourself.

It might be basically what you have on your faculty Web page. if you have one. But go easy on the academic stuff like "presentations and publications." Your page should show who you are more than what you've accomplished. What do you think your students would like to know about you?

139. Go back in time — if you dare.

Faculty tend to think of their personal Web pages as a variant of their CVs, with perhaps a photo and some personal touches, such as a few words about their family and their hobbies. Go beyond the present: add some photos from your past, such as when you were in college ... and maybe when you were in high school or even younger. You could also scan a drawing that you did as a kid. Think of your course Web page not just as a CV but also as a photo album and scrapbook.

140. Assign a "student search."

As students develop their personal pages, consider giving the class an occasional assignment to browse those pages. It should be something simple, with the objective of getting them to visit all of the pages. Ask them to find, for example, a student who was born in Chicago, a student who has a pet ferret, a student who collects stamps, a student who has traveled in South America, and so forth. Collect facts from the personal pages and make them into a scavenger hunt. You can grade the assignments for extra points or simply award prizes to the winners. A few assignments should be enough to serve as a virtual introduction and encourage interest in each other.

141. Adapt "as usual."

If you are like most distance educators in this respect, at this point in this book you're probably already jotting down ideas for adapting "conventional" icebreakers for your situation. Keep in mind your purpose and continue to think of the technology as providing opportunities, not imposing limitations. Use your creativity, your experience, and your instincts!

Category: Miscellaneous

PURPOSE: to make your icebreakers more effective

142. Give prizes.

Some of the icebreakers involve competition and some instructors give prizes to the winners, such as candy, gum, pens or pencils. Small packs of candy can be easy and fun — if you don't mind if the students eat it in class. However, remember that some candy might not work as well; some students may be avoiding peanuts or chocolates, for example, while others may not eat sweets at all. But you can always encourage them to share, which further fosters a sense of community.

143. Don't lose your balance.

One of the first tips in this book was "Balance fun and function." Small prizes can lighten any icebreaker, especially if you have any concerns about students taking it too seriously and competitively. And that's not unlike the suggestion from my cousin, Laura Nicole, to pass out cookies.

144. Start small if the class is large.

It may be difficult to get a sense of community in a large class through a single icebreaker. In classes of more than 20 students, it's generally better to break the class into groups of five or six. Working in groups encourages students to each meet at least four or five of their classmates. That's a good start toward building a sense of community. You might suggest that students within a group exchange e-mail addresses and phone numbers, so they can contact each other if they have questions about assignments (which pages to read, when a paper is due, etc.) or if they want to form study groups.

145. Keep the activity going to keep breaking the ice.

With short icebreakers (5-10 minutes), you may want to use one to start the first three classes, for example, so that each student is grouped with four or five different students each time. The resulting overlap of smaller groups, because each student meets 12 to 15 other students, provides a greater sense of community.

146. Be honest and be real.

If you sense that an icebreaker isn't working well, stop and admit it. That makes sense for several reasons. First, your students have probably already sensed that there's a problem. Second, honesty is the best policy with your students, whatever the situation. Third, your students should appreciate it if you're real with them, if you acknowledge the difficulty and then discuss it. If any of your students had a problem in your course, would you expect any less of them? Instructors who recover well from a difficulty by being honest and real usually gain respect from their students. Katy J. Vopal adds, "But be sure to give it enough time to work — and remember there will always be a student or two who just won't want to do anything."

147. Recognize when the ice is sufficiently broken.

Keep in mind your purpose(s) for using an icebreaker. When your icebreaker has achieved that purpose, end it as smoothly as possible. As one student noted of an icebreaker that went on and on, "We were ready to start learning, but we kept going on with this game, like it was more important than the subject."

Resources!

It would be easy to list books, articles, and Web sites here. But then you would be tempted to go out (physically or virtually) and find some icebreakers: a little research that would not take you outside your comfort zone.

So, to be true to the spirit of this book, I'll close with an icebreaker.

BUILD A LEARNING COMMUNITY ... FOR YOURSELF

Visit, phone, or e-mail 10 colleagues in your field, instructors who teach the same or a similar course. Ask them what icebreakers they've used and which they would recommend. Then, ask each of these colleagues to tell you the five most important things he or she has learned from using icebreakers.

I'll leave you with five final tips, as a bonus.

TIP. Search the Web.

Use your favorite search engine and enter "icebreakers" or "ice breakers" and the subject of your course. You may also need to narrow down the search by including "college." If you don't score some good hits, try searching for words related to your subject matter.

TIP. Ask your students for suggestions.

Your students have a lot of experience with icebreakers — and they can be brutally honest. Take a few moments at the end of the first class and ask them what they thought about the icebreaker you chose. Then, ask them about other icebreakers they know and whether they would have chosen those instead. Not only are you likely to gain some ideas that will help you with your next class, but you'll also be showing the students that you're open to learning from them. This exercise can actually serve as an icebreaker in itself.

TIP. Consult your colleagues.

Talk with other instructors in your field — locally and globally. What icebreakers do they use when they teach online? What have they learned about choosing and using icebreakers? If you expect your students to be learning online from each other, you should be able to do the same.

TIP. Share the wealth.

Create a Web page where instructors in your field can post icebreakers that they have used and would recommend. And feel free to recommend this book!

TIP. Remember: there are no guarantees.

An icebreaker is like any other teaching technique: what works in one class may not work in another — or it may work better.

Please let me know about your experiences with icebreakers. E-mail me at rmagnan@atwoodpublishing.com. Thank you — and good luck!

About the Author

Robert Magnan has plenty of classroom experience after teaching French and English for 13 years at Michigan State University, Indiana University, l'Université de Strasbourg (France), and the University of Wisconsin.

He holds a BA in English and an MA in French from Michigan State University and a PhD in French from Indiana University. Outside of the classroom, he has always been deeply involved in editing, publishing, research, translation, and language-textbook development.

He edited two national newsletters — *The Teaching Professor* and *Professional Scholar* — and written articles for seven other newsletters in higher education — *Student Leader, Perspective: The Campus Legal Monthly, Academic Leader, National On-Campus Report, Recruitment and Retention in Higher Education, Administrator*, and *Quality in Higher Education*.

However, Magnan is best known as the author of the international bestseller *147 Practical Tips for Teaching Professors*, which has been translated into French and Spanish.

He also co-authored, with A. Clay Schoenfeld, a guide for faculty, *Mentor in a Manual: Climbing the Academic Ladder to Tenure*.

He's edited several dozen books, including the following in higher education:

- *Charting Your Course: How to Prepare to Teach More Effectively* by Richard Prégent
- *Contemporary Theories and Practice in Higher Education* by Yves Bertrand
- *First Steps to Excellence in College Teaching* by Glenn Ross Johnson

- *Teaching and Performing: Ideas for Energizing Your Classes* by William M. Timpson, Suzanne Burgoyne, Christine S. Jones, and Waldo Jones
- *Reaching Out: How Campus Leaders Can Communicate More Effectively With Their Constituents* by Clay Schoenfeld and Linda Weimer, in collaboration with Jean M. Lang
- *Learning Style Perspectives: Impact in the Classroom* by Lynne Celli Sarasin
- *Distance Learners in Higher Education: Institutional Responses for Quality Outcomes,* edited by Chère Campbell Gibson